S0-ABP-498

BABY POLAR BEAR

Text copyright © 2008 by Aubrey Lang
Photography copyright © 2008 by Wayne Lynch

Published in Canada by Fitzhenry & Whiteside,
195 Allstate Parkway, Markham, Ontario L3R 4T8

Published in the United States by Fitzhenry & Whiteside,
311 Washington Street, Brighton, Massachusetts 02135

All rights reserved. No part of this book may be reproduced in any manner without the express
written consent of the publisher, except in the case of brief excerpts in critical reviews and articles.
All inquiries should be addressed to Fitzhenry & Whiteside Limited,
195 Allstate Parkway, Markham, Ontario L3R 4T8.

www.fitzhenry.ca godwit@fitzhenry.ca

10 9 8 7 6 5 4 3 2 1

Library and Archives Canada Cataloguing in Publication

Lang, Aubrey
Baby polar bear / Aubrey Lang ; Wayne Lynch (photographer).
(Nature babies)
Includes index.
ISBN 978-1-55455-101-9 (bound).— ISBN 978-1-55455-102-6 (pbk.)
1. Polar bear–Infancy–Juvenile literature.
I. Lynch, Wayne II. Title. III. Series : Lang, Aubrey. Nature babies.
QL737.C27L357 2008   j599.786'139   C2008-902148-7

**U.S. Publisher Cataloging-in-Publication Data
(Library of Congress Standards)**

Lang, Aubrey.
Baby polar bear / Aubrey Lang ; photography by Wayne Lynch.
[36] p. : col. photos. ; cm.   (Nature babies)
Includes index.
Summary: Two polar bear cubs must leave the safety of the den and follow their mother through
the frozen Arctic wilderness as she heads out to the sea ice to hunt for her first meal in many months.
ISBN-13: 978-1-55455-101-9   ISBN-13: 978-1-55455-102-6 (pbk.)
1. Polar bear — Infancy — Juvenile literature. (1. Bears.) I. Lynch, Wayne. II. Title. III. Series.
599.74446 dc22   QL737.C27.L36   2008

Fitzhenry & Whiteside acknowledges with thanks the Canada Council for the Arts, and the Ontario Arts Council
for their support of our publishing program. We acknowledge the financial support of the Government of Canada
through the Book Publishing Industry Development Program (BPIDP) for our publishing activities.

Canada Council Conseil des Arts
for the Arts   du Canada

ONTARIO ARTS COUNCIL
CONSEIL DES ARTS DE L'ONTARIO

Design by Wycliffe Smith Design Inc.
Printed in Singapore

BABY POLAR BEAR

Text by Aubrey Lang

Photography by Wayne Lynch

Fitzhenry & Whiteside

MAIN LIBRARY
Champaign Public Library
200 West Green Street
Champaign, Illinois 61820-5193

BEFORE YOU BEGIN

Hello Young Reader:

To find polar bears, we traveled all across the top of the world. In Russia and Alaska, we sailed on large, powerful ships that can break through thick ice. In Norway, we cruised between the ice floes in rubber boats. Our most exciting adventures were traveling by helicopter in the Canadian Arctic with scientists who were studying the bears. When we camped beside the Arctic Ocean, we sometimes felt nervous sleeping inside a tent, so we surrounded our camp with an electric fence to keep curious polar bears away.

We dedicate this book to the scientists who helped us understand these interesting animals. We especially wish to thank Drs. Ian Stirling and Andrew Derocher.

–Aubrey Lang and Wayne Lynch

TABLE OF CONTENTS

It's snowing sideways. The wind is howling, and the ice on the Arctic Ocean is cracking and groaning. The old female polar bear has lived through many winter blizzards like this. She curls her body into a ball and lets the blowing snow pile up around her. It is so cold that a person's skin would freeze in minutes, but the bear's thick fur keeps her warm.

Three days later, the storm has passed. The bear is hungry and eager to hunt.

The female polar bear spends most of the year on the frozen ocean. The sea water under the ice is always moving. This movement breaks the ice into large pieces. Sometimes the pieces crash together, and the ice is pushed up into steep hills. Other times, the pieces float apart and create cracks and pools of open water. This cold and icy world is the polar bear's home.

The polar bear is a strong swimmer. Her front paws are the size of dinner plates, and they make perfect paddles. She has a long neck, so it is easy to keep her head above the water. The fat under her skin helps her stay warm. Her furry feet are like a pair of warm slippers. When she walks on the ice, her sharp claws keep her from slipping.

It is early spring when male and female polar bears come together to start a family. A large male bear sees some tracks in the snow and smells them. The tracks belong to the female bear, and he follows her, trailing her for several days. Slowly the male gets closer. Finally one day, the two bears meet and play together.

He will be the father of her cubs.

A week later, the male leaves. The mother bear will raise her cubs alone. Now that she is pregnant, she must catch many seals. She will become as fat as she can so she'll have lots of milk for her babies later.

It is a good time of the year for hunting. There are many young seals on the ice.

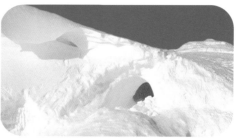

The mother hunts all summer long and gets very fat.
When winter finally arrives, she returns to the land to
dig a snow house, called a den. On Christmas Day, the
mother bear gives birth to a male and female cub.
When the babies are born, they are no bigger than
chubby chipmunks.

The family stays inside the den for several months. At
last the cubs are big enough to come outside.

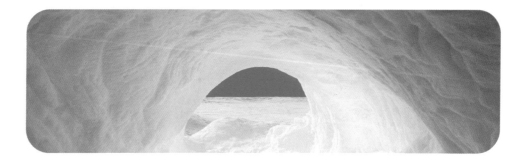

The family spends a week near the winter den. Here the young bears will get stronger every day. The cubs tumble and play. Even when the mother tries to snooze, the healthy young bears climb all over her.

The mother has not eaten for almost six months. Soon she will return to the ice to hunt again.

The sea ice is far away. It's a long walk when your legs are short. The mother bear is very patient, and she stops often to let her small cubs rest. The little female cub is stronger than her brother; she doesn't tire as quickly. Sometimes the mother lets the male cub ride on her back.

During the long walk to the
frozen ocean, the cubs meet
some neighbors. A snowy
owl frightens them when it
suddenly flies overhead.
The family accidentally
disturbs a sleeping arctic
hare. Even the mother

jumps back in surprise when the big, bouncing bunny
leaps out of its hole.

What the cubs don't know is that an arctic fox is following
them to the ice. The clever animal hopes to grab some
tasty leftovers after the hunt.

After several days of walking, the polar bear family reaches the jumble of ice along the edge of the ocean. The mother wants to hunt, but her cubs are tired and need to rest.

The mother is worried about other polar bears that hunt in this area. Big male bears will sometimes attack and kill baby bears, so the mother is always watching, smelling, and listening for danger.

One day, the mother sniffs a smelly bearded seal. She tries to sneak closer to the snoozing seal, but the cubs just want to play. They scare the seal into the water.

In the weeks to come, the cubs will learn to stay quiet and still. By watching their mother's every move, they will also learn how to hunt.

Big, blubbery walruses also live along the edge of the ice. They are the biggest animals that polar bears hunt. The walruses smell the bear family coming and escape into the water. But with her small cubs nearby, the mother bear has no intention of hunting these dangerous animals.

To the young bears, the big walruses are just noisy and scary. And their breath smells like stinky clams.

The summer is over, and the cold, dark days of winter will soon arrive. The baby bears have been eating meat for many months. Even so, they still need their mother's rich, fatty milk to stay healthy. Because  the mother bear is such a good hunter, she can produce lots of thick milk for her cubs to drink.

It will take some time for the young polar bears to become good enough hunters to live on their own. The bears will spend two more winters with their mother. They will finally leave her when they are two and a half years old. The valuable hunting lessons they have learned from their mother will help them survive in their frozen world.

DID YOU KNOW?

- Polar bears are found only in the northern polar world. There are no polar bears in the southern polar world of Antarctica, where penguins live.

- Air pollution has caused the Earth's temperature to warm up. The temperature is rising fastest in the Arctic. If this warming trend continues, the arctic pack ice may disappear completely during the summer months. Without ice, polar bears cannot hunt. Scientists worry that the bears may be unable to survive.

- Polar bears are carnivores, or meat eaters. They mainly hunt the small ringed seal and the much larger bearded seal. Occasionally, they prey on walruses and white beluga whales.

- Polar bears range in color from silvery white to a light yellow. Cubs are always pure white, but some bears, especially adult males, turn yellow as they get older.

- Female polar bears usually have their first litter of cubs when they are five years old. After that, they may have a new set of cubs every three years. Typically, they give birth to one or two cubs at a time. A mother bear could raise up to twelve cubs during her lifetime.

- Many polar bears can hunt throughout the winter, so they do not need to hibernate like black bears and grizzly bears do. Pregnant polar bears are the exception. They dig a winter den to give birth to their cubs.

- On average, polar bears are the largest of all the bears. Adult males weigh between 650 and 1540 pounds (300-700 kilograms). Standing on all fours, a large male bear may be 5 feet (1.5 meters) tall at the shoulder. On its hind legs, it can stand as tall as 11 feet (3.5 meters). Female bears are usually half the size of males.

INDEX

BIOGRAPHIES

Aubrey Lang and Dr. Wayne Lynch are a husband and wife writer/photographer team. Aubrey has spent the past eighteen years as a freelance writer and photographer. Wayne has been a full-time science writer and wildlife photographer for twenty-eight years. His images have been published in more than three dozen

countries. Together they've produced more than forty-five titles for children and adults, as well as scripts for television documentaries and countless articles in well-known nature magazines, including *Ranger Rick, Owl, Wild, National Wildlife, Wildlife Conservation, Canadian Geographic,* and *Canadian Wildlife.*